How Church Could (Literally) Save Your Life

Other Gospel Coalition Books

Confronting Christianity: 12 Hard Questions for the World's Largest Religion, by Rebecca McLaughlin

Confronting Jesus: 9 Encounters with the Hero of the Gospels, by Rebecca McLaughlin

Did the Resurrection Really Happen?, by Timothy Paul Jones

Questioning Faith: Indirect Journeys of Belief Through Terrains of Doubt, by Randy Newman

Rediscover Church: Why the Body of Christ Is Essential, by Collin Hansen and Jonathan Leeman

Remember Death: The Surprising Path to Living Hope, by Matthew McCullough

What Does Depression Mean for My Faith?, by Kathryn Butler, MD

Where Is God in a World with So Much Evil?, by Collin Hansen

Why Do We Feel Lonely at Church?, by Jeremy Linneman

To explore all titles from the Gospel Coalition, including those in the New City Catechism, TGC Kids, and TGC Hard Questions lines, visit TGC.org/books.

"The empirical research on religion and health could be seen as an invitation back to communal religious life for those who (for a range of reasons) are not currently part of a faith community. Rebecca McLaughlin issues that invitation in a most compelling manner."

Tyler VanderWeele, Professor of Epidemiology, Harvard School of Public Health; Director of the Human Flourishing Program, Harvard University

"In medical practice, doctors often suggest that diagnosis is easy but therapy is difficult. Rebecca McLaughlin challenges this assertion. Here she reviews the scientific evidence and proposes a treatment for our physical and psychological woes that is readily available, efficacious, and free of charge. Best of all, you don't need a doctor's prescription. The question for us all is this: Will we trust the data and swallow the pill?"

Lydia S. Dugdale, MD, Dorothy L. and Daniel H. Silberberg Professor of Medicine, Columbia University Medical Center; author, *The Lost Art of Dying: Reviving Forgotten Wisdom*

"In an era of dechurching, this book surprises with emerging evidence that going to church has significant benefits. But there is more at stake here than our physical and mental health. Engaging understandable doubts, McLaughlin shows how Jesus helps us understand ourselves and our world—and offers nothing less than ultimate healing."

John R. Peteet, MD, Associate Professor of Psychiatry, Harvard Medical School

"A wonderful little book. Rebecca McLaughlin makes a powerful case for the mental, physical, moral, and spiritual benefits of going to church, blending scientific research with personal stories and wise application."

Andrew Wilson, Teaching Pastor, King's Church London

"Rebecca McLaughlin functions a bit like an oracle to me—her work is consistently on point and timely; her instincts point true gospel north. For centuries, Christians have claimed that following Jesus leads to life and happiness. This helpful book shows that even modern social science is beginning to say, 'Yes and amen!' Characteristic of Rebecca's style, this book is carefully researched and evenly reasoned. Whether preparing a talk, talking with a friend, or teaching your kids, you'll undoubtedly find yourself turning to it again and again."

J. D. Greear, Pastor, The Summit Church, Raleigh-Durham, North Carolina; author, *Everyday Revolutionary: How to Transcend the Culture War and Transform the World*

"This data-rich, clear case for attending church confirms that we were made to worship. In McLaughlin's final prescription we find the ultimate reason to attend church: Christ. For the skeptic or the waning churchgoer, this well-written and deeply researched book will inspire."

Alan Noble, Professor of English, Oklahoma Baptist University; author, *On Getting Out of Bed*

"We can be quick to criticize the church, both its structures and its people, without fully considering what we lose by avoiding it. In this concise and thoughtful book, Rebecca McLaughlin makes a compelling case for how regular participation in a local church profoundly impacts our mental, physical, moral, and spiritual well-being. Backed by substantive research, she invites readers to take an honest look at the long-term impact of staying away and reminds us of the lifesaving strength and flourishing found in worshiping with other believers week after week."

Elizabeth Woodson, Bible teacher; podcaster; author, *Embrace Your Life*; *From Beginning to Forever*; and *Live Free*

How Church Could (Literally) Save Your Life

Rebecca McLaughlin

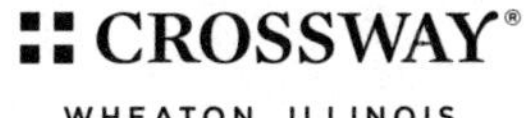

WHEATON, ILLINOIS

How Church Could (Literally) Save Your Life

Published by Crossway
1300 Crescent Street
Wheaton, Illinois 60187

Cover image: Getty Images

Cover design: David Fassett

First printing 2025

Printed in the United States of America

Trade paperback ISBN: 978-1-4335-9969-9
ePub ISBN: 978-1-4335-9971-2
PDF ISBN: 978-1-4335-9970-5

Library of Congress Cataloging-in-Publication Data

Names: McLaughlin, Rebecca, 1980– author

Title: How church could (literally) save your life / Rebecca McLaughlin.

Description: Wheaton, Illinois : Crossway, [2025] | Series: The Gospel coalition | Includes bibliographical references and index.

Identifiers: LCCN 2025006500 (print) | LCCN 2025006501 (ebook) | ISBN 9781433599699 trade paperback | ISBN 9781433599705 pdf | ISBN 9781433599712 epub

Subjects: LCSH: Church attendance | Mission of the church—United States | Mind and body—Religious aspects—Christianity | Mental health—Religious aspects—Christianity | Church attendance—United States

Classification: LCC BV4523 .M455 2025 (print) | LCC BV4523 (ebook) | DDC 264—dc23/eng/20250430

LC record available at https://lccn.loc.gov/2025006500

LC ebook record available at https://lccn.loc.gov/2025006501

Crossway is a publishing ministry of Good News Publishers.

VP 34 33 32 31 30 29 28 27 26 25
15 14 13 12 11 10 9 8 7 6 5 4 3 2 1

Contents

Introduction

IMAGINE THIS BOOK filled with pills instead of pages. You open it and fifty-two neatly laid out tablets meet your eyes. If you're young and healthy, you might think, *I don't need these.* You either throw them out or stash them in a box somewhere for future use. If you're older or suffer from chronic physical or mental illness, you may be more intrigued. What if this is just the medication you're looking for?

This book isn't a pillbox. But it does contain a prescription. The script is for something that—if taken at least weekly—could elongate your life expectancy by seven years, significantly increase your chance of happiness, and substantially reduce the likelihood you'll suffer from depression.

Thinking this is too good to be true, you check for side effects. They're listed as a greater sense of meaning, greater likelihood of volunteering, and more generosity toward those in need. Once again, you're skeptical. This must be a scam.

You turn to the back cover to see where this information comes from. There you find this medication has been extensively tested by none other than the Harvard School of Public Health.

Would you take the pills?

In a 2016 article for *USA Today*, Harvard School of Public Health Professor Tyler VanderWeele and journalist John Siniff posed this question:

> If one could conceive of a single elixir to improve the physical and mental health of millions of Americans—at no personal cost—what value would our society place on it?
>
> Going a step further, if research quite conclusively showed that when consumed just once a week, this concoction would reduce mortality by 20% to 30% over a 15-year period, how urgently would we want to make it publicly available?[1]

Professor VanderWeele is director of the human flourishing program at Harvard. He's a literal world expert on what's good for you and me. So, what's this magic potion he's found?

We may think VanderWeele has conjured up a health-enhancing drug. Perhaps he's found a side-effect-free diet pill? Or some safe substance that will make you want to exercise? Or maybe yoga, meditation, or some novel super-food? But VanderWeele goes on: "The good news is that this miracle drug—religion, and more specifically regular church attendance—is already in reach of most Americans. In fact, there's a good chance it's just a short drive away."

Whatever your beliefs, my guess is that you wouldn't expect a Harvard professor to write you this prescription: "Church. Take once a week (or more) for best effects." But study after study has shown that people who attend religious services once a week or more are happier, healthier, and longer-lived than those who don't. If any other practice had the same effects, it would be widely advertised in public health campaigns.

I wonder how that information lands for you.

Many today see church as outdated, unnecessary, or even harmful. Maybe you identify as "spiritual, but not religious." You'd rather climb a mountain or gaze up at the stars than go to church. Perhaps you've been put off by racism, abuse, hypocrisy, or hateful attitudes. Church is the last place you would want to show up on a Sunday. Perhaps you grew up in a different religious tradition. At this point, you don't regularly attend religious services, but it would feel offensive for someone to invite you to church. Or maybe you identify as atheist, agnostic, or "nothing in particular," and your first thought on hearing about the benefits of church is that they must be explained by community support. If one of these describes you, I'm honored you'd take time to read this book. You're likely someone who thinks carefully and wants to see the data before you make a decision. My hope is that the data in this book will give you food for thought.

Maybe you feel less skeptical and more wistful when you hear talk of church. Perhaps you weren't raised in church, but you've seen how meaningful it is to other people, and you feel a little robbed. Perhaps you used to go to church, but then you moved to a new city and haven't found a new church. Perhaps you stopped attending during COVID and never quite got back into the habit. Perhaps you went through a divorce, or changed your job, or your kids had Sunday morning soccer games, and church just quietly slid off your weekly calendar. Perhaps you're single and the church you went to seemed to revolve around married couples. Maybe you found yourself out of step with others at your church politically and you stopped attending. Or you became depressed or struggle with anxiety, and making it to church on Sundays just feels too hard.

If one of these scenarios describes you, you're not alone. These are some of the reasons why, in the first quarter of the twenty-first century, forty million Americans (around 12 percent of the population) have stopped attending church.[2] If you don't see yourself as a religious person, you might think this is good news. Many think that less religion means less bigotry and more happy, psychologically healthy, socially responsible citizens. But the results of what has been called "the great dechurching" in America have been measurably bad. Less churchgoing has led to lower mental health and happiness, more loneliness, more drug abuse, more alcoholism, less volunteering, less giving to those in need, reduced life expectancy, and more suicides. Even the most skeptical experts acknowledge that declining church attendance in the United States and (over a longer time period) across the West has had devastating side effects.

In chapters 1 and 2 of this short book, we'll reckon with the data on the mental and physical health benefits of weekly church attendance. We'll see that these effects can't be explained away simply by social contact. As VanderWeele explains, "Social support is critical, yet this accounts for only about a quarter of the effect."[3] The majority of religious-service participants in the studies have been churchgoers, but most studies don't differentiate between different kinds of religious services. So, for instance, people going to Jewish synagogues once a week or more report benefits similar to those attending Christian churches. But the religious element seems to be vital. Parents who join the same people each week to cheer for their kids' sports team won't see the same level of benefit. We humans seem to thrive when we worship together.

In chapter 3, we'll look at the moral effects of going to church each week. However you identify religiously, my guess is that you see altruism (whether in the form of giving money or volunteering time to charitable causes) as beneficial for society. So we'll examine the effects someone's religious practices have on how they treat those most in need. We'll also ask a deeper question: Why do we think caring for the poor, sick, and vulnerable is good? This may seem like a strange question. But whether we realize it or not, it turns out that the seemingly self-evident truth that all human life is equally valuable—regardless of a person's age, sex, nationality, income level, or abilities—came to us from Christianity. If Christianity isn't true, we aren't left with a better secular foundation for our core belief that all humans are equal. We're left with that ethical rug pulled out from underneath our feet.

Finally, in chapter 4, we'll face the truth that haunts all of our lives. However healthy you and I may be—however much we work out, eat well, sleep, don't smoke, get annual health checks, or even go to church—we'll all end up as corpses before long. So, in this book's last chapter, we'll look at Christianity's wild claim that anyone who puts her or his trust in Jesus will be carried right through death to everlasting life with him. You may think this is simply not believable today. But VanderWeele is one of many world-class scholars who would challenge that assumption. Rather than dismissing Christianity out of hand, VanderWeele suggests that "any educated person should, at some point, have critically examined the claims for Christianity and should be able to explain why he or she does, or does not, believe them."

If you've never been to church with any regularity before, my hope is that this book will make you want to try it out. If you were once a regular attender, perhaps you'll think of coming back. On the last page, you'll find a website and a QR code that will help you get connected to a church in your area, and you'll see a list of questions frequently asked by those considering going to church (What can I expect? What should I wear? etc.).

If you hate church and everything it stands for, I'm thankful you've read this far. I wrote another book especially for you. It's called *Confronting Christianity*, and it looks at twelve of the biggest reasons you may have for not considering the Christian faith. If you find this book even slightly thought-provoking, maybe you'll read that one too.

If you're not sure what to believe, but you need more hope and love and meaning in your life, my prayer is that this book will function as an invitation to look for a local church where you could find out more about who Jesus is and maybe start attending regularly. If church is, as VanderWeele claims, something of a "miracle drug," why not start popping that pill now?

1

Mental Health Benefits

YESTERDAY, I TOOK A YOUNG FRIEND out to lunch to celebrate her one-year anniversary of joining our church. She wasn't raised in church, and like many Gen Zers, she tried a range of spiritual practices to fill that hole. She tried astrology, bought tarot cards, used crystals, and engaged in meditation. But nothing seemed to satisfy. She turned to substances to help her cope with life, bingeing on alcohol, smoking pot, and vaping. But none of these gave more than short-term fixes. She tried relationships with men and then with women, worked a range of different kinds of jobs, and lived on different continents. But all her various experiments left her feeling empty. Knowing she was struggling with mental health, she found a therapist and started taking antidepressants. But still her nagging sense of meaninglessness continued, chipping away at her ability to flourish. It wasn't until she turned to Jesus and began attending church on Sundays and mid-week Bible studies that life started to make sense.

The details of my young friend's story are unique. But its broad contours are not. Many in the West today attempt to fill in their spiritual gap with New Age practices, a range of sexual relationships, and substance use. More people are in therapy and on antidepressants than at any other time. And yet our mental health across the West has nose-dived. As we'll see in this chapter, all our freedom to experiment and self-define without constraints has bred more misery than happiness. And one of the best things we can do to boost our mental health is what my friend eventually did: commit to church.

Diagnosis

Since you're reading this, I'm willing to bet that either you've struggled with significant depression or you love someone who has. The new millennium has seen a surge in depression, anxiety, and suicidal ideation across the West. Between 2015 and 2023 in the United States, the proportion of adults diagnosed with depression at some point in their lives went up by almost 10 percentage points to 29 percent. In the same period, the proportion of people who have been or are currently being treated for depression went up by 7 points to

17.8 percent.[1] We've removed much of the shame and stigma once associated with mental health struggles. But we haven't succeeded in reducing the struggles. Instead, they've spread like an oil spill, entrapping more and more of us like seagulls with our wings weighed down.

As my young friend experienced, this mental health disaster has hit women hardest. We see ourselves as living in the most pro-woman culture in all human history. Yet women in our culture are increasingly unhappy. Thirty-seven percent of women now report being diagnosed with depression at some point in their lives, compared with 20 percent of men.[2] The mental health crisis has also been particularly hard on younger people. In 2023, 27.3 percent of girls and 9.4 percent of boys ages twelve to seventeen reported experiencing a major depressive episode in the past year, more than double the rates in 2004.[3] Likewise, between 2009 and 2021, the share of American high school students who said they had "persistent feelings of sadness or hopelessness" rose from 26 percent to 44 percent.[4] Tragically, between 2007 and 2021, the suicide rate among ten-to-twenty-four-year-olds also increased by 62 percent.[5]

So, what's driving this depression and despair?

We might look to COVID to shoulder the blame. The effects of the social isolation bred by the pandemic are certainly profound. But as one 2022 report points out, depression was "an escalating public health crisis" in the United States before we had ever even heard of COVID.[6]

One cause of the mental health crisis is the rise of smartphones and social media, which have driven isolation, negative comparison, and the social contagion of a host of mental health conditions. Again, women and young people have been most affected. By 2023, the evidence for the dangers of smartphone and social-media use for children and adolescents was so clear that the US surgeon general issued an official public health warning.[7] But smartphones can't take all the blame.

Another factor undermining mental health is the decline in marriage. Many nonreligious people think increased societal acceptance of sex outside marriage leads to better mental health and greater happiness. But the data tells a different tale. For women in particular, increased numbers of sexual partners correlates with more depression, sadness, and suicidal ideation, and increased likelihood of substance abuse. Marriage has the opposite effect.[8] After analyzing data from a large-scale, long-term survey, University of Chicago Professor Sam Peltzman noted, "Being married is the most important differentiator with a 30-percentage point happy–unhappy gap over the unmarried."[9] Likewise, research conducted by the Institute for Family Studies found that "married people are approximately 16% more likely than unmarried people to describe their mental health as 'excellent' or 'very good' within every category of formal education."[10] Marriage, it turns out, functions less like a restrictive straitjacket and more like a protective seat belt.

But alongside the astronomic growth in smartphone use and the decline in marriage, it's increasingly clear that one major driver of the mental health crisis is the decline in church attendance.

Prescription

Even if you haven't seen Disney's *Encanto*, the song "We Don't Talk About Bruno" probably lives somewhere in the basement of your mind. In this song, the Madrigal family tells Maribel about her uncle Bruno, who disappeared some years ago. The Madrigals mistakenly believe Bruno caused a host of bad things he prophesied. That song came to my mind just now as I clicked on link after link to articles with titles promising the "Top 10 Mental Health Hacks" or something similar. I wondered whether any would mention going to church. None did. You can try the exercise yourself.

Psychologists are keen to let us know how exercise, good sleep, and eating healthy foods can boost our mental health and happiness. They advocate yoga, mindfulness, and meditation. But like the awkward uncle we're all trying to forget, we don't talk about "organized religion."

Like Bruno in his family's perception, church often has negative associations. We've all heard stories of people who at last felt free to be themselves when they left church behind. Maybe that was your experience. What's more, in a culture that promotes self-love, unbounded freedom, and the good of always following our hearts, some Christian teachings—like the idea that many of our deep desires are sinful—seem like they'd be bad for mental health and happiness. Before she turned to Jesus, the young friend I mentioned earlier had a mug that said, "Nobody's perfect. I'm nobody." But when she finally became convinced that Christianity is true, one thing that brought relief was the new understanding of herself the Bible gives. Whereas she'd tried to believe she was basically good, the Christian message gave her tools to recognize the many ways she was in fact quite bad. At the same time, her newfound faith gave her deep confidence she is loved by the Creator God of all the universe, who sent his Son to die for her.

Many in our culture think prioritizing self-love and rejecting the uncomfortable beliefs that come with Christianity will lead to happiness. But the evidence is quite the opposite. Going to church weekly actually is one of the best protections against depression, sadness, and suicidal ideation anyone has found. A 2022 analysis of studies showed "a roughly 33 percent reduction in the odds of subsequent depression for those attending services at least weekly versus not at all."[11] In other words, if you aren't currently a churchgoer and you start attending weekly, you reduce your chances of developing depression by a third.

A medication this effective would be widely prescribed. But while your therapist or doctor may encourage yoga, meditation, or more time outside in nature, he or she almost certainly won't recommend you go to church. The benefits of "organized religion" don't fit with the big story we are telling in the West about the goodness of abandoning traditional beliefs. So, despite the studies showing how good religious services can be for people's mental health, we don't talk about Bruno.

Can these positive effects be explained away because those battling depression are less likely to have energy for church? That's a great question. The answer is no. Studies have controlled for baseline depressive symptoms and found that church really is making a difference. If you're currently depressed, the thought of getting out of bed on Sunday morning and heading to a church can feel completely overwhelming. Especially if you don't already have a church community, the idea of going to a place where you don't yet know people—and might not know the songs they'll sing or prayers they'll pray—may feel like a steep hill to climb. I've had friends struggling with depression share the difficulty of making it to church.

But evidence shows that attending each week is more like a life rope—even if it takes a lot of effort to grab hold and cling on. Not only do churchgoers cut their chances of depression by a third; depressed people who attend church weekly also have a significantly better chance of recovering than those who don't.[12] Instead of dragging you still further down into depression, church could be just what you need to pull you out. But like any other medication, you'll need to stay the course to see the positive effects.

You may read this and think, *You just don't get it. I've been hurt by church.* Maybe you've experienced hypocrisy, judgmental attitudes, or even terrible abuse. I know people who've been profoundly hurt in church and who bear scars of pain and disillusionment from the experience. Just as our families can be the places of greatest love and of most horrific pain, so church can be a place of safety or of harm. But just as growing up in an unhealthy family wouldn't lead you to give up on family for good, so the experience of an unhealthy church need not mean giving up on church. A genuinely loving, healthy church may be just what you need to heal. Indeed, it can be literally lifesaving.

When it comes to the devastating topic of suicide, the difference between those who regularly attend religious services and those who never do is stark. Professor VanderWeele's research has found that women who never attend religious services are *five times more likely* to end their own lives than those who attend weekly or more.[13] I was so stunned when I first read this study that I emailed VanderWeele to ask if it was really representative. He responded that it was not an outlier. Indeed, VanderWeele has estimated that "approximately 40% of the rise in suicide rates between 1999 and 2014 may be attributable to declining service attendance."[14]

To be clear, this doesn't make churchgoers immune to suicidal ideation any more than they're immune to depression more generally. One of our church members who attends and serves faithfully struggles with chronic suicidal ideation and has appropriately sought both medical and spiritual help. But any honest suicide prevention campaign ought to include a recommendation to try attending religious services. It's one of the best protections against suicide anyone has found.

So, is church like an antidepressant—good for people struggling with mental health but quite unnecessary for those who aren't? No. Worshiping alongside others seems not only to protect us from emotional distress but also to increase our happiness. A 2019 report found that in the United States, 36 percent of adults who go to church regularly describe themselves as "very happy," compared with just 25 percent of adults who identify as religious but don't go to church or who don't identify with any one religion. This phenomenon isn't unique to the United States. In Australia, for instance, 45 percent of churchgoing adults say they are very happy, compared with 33 percent of those who are religiously unaffiliated.[15] People who go to church each week tend to feel happier, enjoy higher life satisfaction, and have more of a sense of purpose than those who don't. They're also more optimistic about the future and have more self-control.[16]

Again, this data doesn't fit the modern Western script. We're taught that organized religion, with its talk of sin and self-denial, is a drain on human happiness. We're urged to live our dreams and find our bliss, like solo voyagers charting our own course to satisfaction. But like a little rowboat ill-equipped to make it on the sea, we're far more likely to get shipwrecked if we aim for happiness on our own. Joining a large crew with a greater purpose and mission—one defined not by self-fulfillment but by love of God and others—turns out to be better for our mental health and happiness.

A few months after she'd joined our church, the young friend I mentioned earlier volunteered for our annual Christmas tree giveaway, which features a live-animal petting zoo in the church building. After the giveaway, my friend and I were part of the cleaning crew, and she was tasked with mopping up the goat pee that had leaked onto the floor. "Welcome to the Christian life!" I quipped. She replied, "I'm having the best time!" The mission of serving other people arm-in-arm with friends is a vital element of Christian ethics. It's also powerfully tied to human flourishing.

If you, like me, are raising kids, I have no doubt you want them to grow into happy, healthy, caring grown-ups. If you had a religious upbringing you hated, or if you weren't raised religious, you may think keeping your kids away from church will give them better odds of flourishing. But once again, the data says the opposite. Taking our kids to church each week is one of the best things we can do for both their present and their future mental health and happiness. In fact, VanderWeele suggests that "declining [service] attendance from 1991 to 2019 accounted for 28 percent of the increase in depression among adolescents."[17]

As a mother of two adolescent girls, I'm heartbroken over the mental health crisis in their demographic. I see so many fellow parents feeling helpless as their kids spiral off into depression or anxiety. This horror can strike even the most church-invested family. Nonetheless, the data shows that one of the best things we can do to protect our children's mental health is to take them to church once a week or more. The evidence is so strong that in 2019, therapist Erica Komisar wrote a *Wall Street Journal* article titled "Don't Believe in God? Lie to Your Children." Komisar began, "As a therapist, I'm often asked to explain why depression and anxiety are so common among children and adolescents. One of the most important explanations—and perhaps the most neglected—is declining interest in religion."[18]

A few months ago, I sat next to a fellow Brit on a plane. She told me she'd recently found her six-year-old son in tears. When she asked what was wrong, her son asked, "What's the point of life if we're just going to die someday?" She told me the question had shaken her, because she knew she didn't have an answer. Many parents in the West today have stopped encouraging their kids to believe in God and focused on telling them to believe in themselves. But deep down, children know they cannot be the center of their universe. Over time, they come to feel less like shining stars and more like they're being sucked into a black hole.

The positive effects of being raised in church can last long after children have left home. In 2018, VanderWeele and his colleague Dr. Ying Chen published results from a study that followed five thousand adolescents over an eight-year period.

Their study found that a religious upbringing contributed to a host of positive health and well-being outcomes later in life. For instance, people raised attending services at least weekly are 18 percent more likely to report high levels of happiness as young adults (ages twenty-three to thirty), 12 percent less likely to have high depressive symptoms, and 33 percent less likely to use illegal drugs. Kids raised in church also go on to have a greater sense of life satisfaction and more purpose, are more likely to forgive others, and are more likely to volunteer.[19] What's more, a 2012 study found that children who regularly attended religious services were 40 percent more likely to graduate from high school and 70 percent more likely to go to college than their non-churchgoing peers.[20] Reporting on one large-scale study, Chen concluded, "Many children are raised religiously, and our study shows that this can powerfully affect their health behaviors, mental health, and overall happiness and well-being."[21]

Directions for Use

As I've mentioned, none of this research means those who go to church each week can't struggle with severe, ongoing mental health challenges. My friend Alan Noble has written a helpful book for Christians who (like him) struggle profoundly. It's titled *On Getting Out of Bed: The Burden and Gift of Living*. At times, Christians have set a harmful expectation that believers shouldn't suffer from depression or anxiety—or that if they do, they should only turn to Scripture, prayer, and the church for help. But throughout the last two thousand years, some of the most influential Christians have had major mental health challenges. For instance, the nineteenth-century English preacher Charles Spurgeon, who was an incredibly powerful communicator of the good news about Jesus, had bouts of deep depression. "I pity a dog who has to suffer what I have," Spurgeon reflected.[22]

Christians who experience depression should be encouraged to seek clinical and spiritual help. "Do not think it unspiritual to remember that you have a body," Spurgeon remarked. "The physician is often as needful as the minister." Having a full range of options for support is helpful, especially for those who have experienced abuse and other kinds of devastating trauma. Yet therapy and medications won't provide the true community and purpose we all need.

The Christian life directs our eyes away from self-fulfillment, self-belief, or self-love and toward to one who gave his life for love of us and calls us to lay down our lives for one another (1 John 3:16). It means we must put others first, and sometimes it means mopping up the goat pee on the floor. As my young friend experienced firsthand, the evidence that church is good for mental health is undeniable. But like most medical prescriptions, it comes with directions for use: take once a week or more.

2

Physical Health Benefits

"PEOPLE ARE LOOKING for the magic pill . . . and the magic pill is already here."

These words from Luigi Ferrucci, MD, the scientific director of the National Institute on Aging, were featured in a 2024 *New York Times* article by journalist Dana Smith titled "The 7 Keys to Longevity." People in our modern world are increasingly desperate to live long and healthy lives. The less hope we have of life beyond the grave, the more we grasp at any promise of life-lengthening and health-enhancing interventions. But Smith attempts to bring us back to basics. "Ignore the hyperbaric chambers and infrared light," she urges. "These are the evidence-backed secrets to aging well:"

1. Move more.
2. Eat more fruits and vegetables.
3. Get enough sleep.
4. Don't smoke, and don't drink too much either.
5. Manage your chronic conditions.
6. Prioritize your relationships.
7. Cultivate a positive mindset.[1]

These are all healthy practices. But like almost every other listicle you'll find online, this article leaves out one of the most robustly evidence-backed practices we can adopt to maximize our chances to live long and healthy lives: Go to church.

Diagnosis

In 1900, people born in the United States could reasonably expect to live for forty-seven years—though if they made it through their first five, they might get well beyond that not-so-ripe old age.[2] By 2000, life expectancy was up to 76.6, and therapeutic breakthroughs were still streaming in. My grandpa died of prostate cancer in his fifties. It was 1985. If his cancer had struck two decades later, he'd likely have had better treatment and survived.

Between 2000 and 2010, life expectancy in the United States rose two years more to 78.7. But in the decade following, the rate of progress trailed off. In 2019, it stood at 78.8 years, a tiny increase for nine years of medical advances.[3] In 2021, thanks to the pandemic, life expectancy decreased to 76. While it bounced back somewhat to 77.5 in 2022, it still isn't trending up as one might expect with all the therapeutic progress we see year over year. In the United Kingdom, where I come from, life expectancy has also stalled. Multiple factors have contributed to this. Almost all go hand in hand with decreased church attendance.

In 2023, US Surgeon General Vivek Murthy called loneliness "an underappreciated public health crisis."[4] The same alarms are being sounded in my homeland. "Britain is in a loneliness epidemic," one 2024 headline explained, "and young people are at the heart of it."[5] The mental health effects of loneliness are obvious. But as Murthy points out, there are substantial physical health costs too.

> The physical health consequences of poor or insufficient connection include a 29% increased risk of heart disease, a 32% increased risk of stroke, and a 50% increased risk of developing dementia for older adults. Additionally, lacking social connection increases risk of premature death by more than 60%.[6]

Murthy acknowledges the evidence that loneliness has risen as churchgoing has declined.[7] But "lack of church attendance" isn't written on anyone's death certificate. So, what is?

The top two causes of death in the West are heart disease and cancer. Along with genetic predisposition, smoking, drinking, and obesity are among the most substantial risk factors. In America, lung cancer kills more people than any other type, and nearly nine out of ten lung-cancer deaths are linked to smoking cigarettes or to secondhand exposure. Smoking also increases the risk of most other kinds of cancer,[8] and it's a major risk factor for heart disease.[9] Thankfully, smoking has become less prevalent in the United States. While 42.4 percent of US adults smoked in 1965, by 2022 only 19.8 percent reported using tobacco products. Rates of smoking among younger Americans saw significant decline even in the decade between 2011 and 2022.[10] But while younger people are less likely to smoke, they're more likely to abuse drugs and alcohol, and an increasing number of younger people in America are dying so-called "deaths of despair"—deaths caused by suicide, drug abuse, or alcohol. Tragically, the proportion of Americans who died deaths of despair doubled between 2000 and 2017.[11]

This heartbreaking increase in deaths of despair can be seen in all three categories. The first two decades of this century saw the suicide rate in America increase by 32 percent, making suicide the second leading cause of death for people ages ten to thirty-four.[12] The number of people who died from a drug overdose in 2021 was more than six times the number in 1999,[13] with over 932,000 Americans dying in this way between 1999 and 2020.[14] Meanwhile, alcohol-related deaths have grown by 30 percent in recent years.[15] The pandemic triggered a particular surge, but rates were increasing prior to that crisis. As a 2024 article explains, "Excessive drinking is responsible for nearly 500 U.S. deaths every day, whether from car accidents, liver disease, or dozens of other risks. An estimated 1 in 8 deaths among U.S. adults ages 20 to 64 each year is attributable to excessive drinking."[16]

What could help to turn this tragic tide?

Prescription

People sometimes think of church as a retirement plan: potentially important late in life, but not worth bothering with until your hair turns gray. Yet the positive effects of church on health kick in early. One large-scale study found that those attending services more than weekly at age twenty had a roughly seven-year greater life expectancy than their non-churchgoing peers.[17]

If you're well beyond your twenties and you're wondering if it's still worth trying church, the answer is a deafening yes! For comparison, annual mammograms are recommended for women from age forty because early breast cancer detection can save lives. But if you're a woman over forty, weekly churchgoing has almost the exact same effect on your longevity as annual mammograms.[18] Drawing on data from multiple studies, VanderWeele estimates that weekly church attendance correlates with a 20–30 percent less chance of dying over a fifteen-year period. One large-scale study that informed this estimate found that women who attended religious services more than once per week had a 33 percent lower likelihood of dying in the sixteen-year follow-up period, compared with women who never attended.[19]

If we look back to the seven evidence-backed keys to longevity reported in the *New York Times*, we'll see that religious service attendance really should have made the list. Attending church each week has almost exactly the same effect on your odds of dying in the next ten years as eating more fruits and vegetables, which came in at number 2. It has almost as much of a positive effect as starting to exercise or quitting smoking, which were numbers 1 and 4.[20] If you (like me) struggle to exercise regularly, or if you have a smoking habit, you could start going to church to offset the effects of your otherwise unhealthy life! But church will also help you kick unhealthy habits.

Most smokers want to stop. But it's hard. One survey found that 85 percent of smokers have tried to quit at least once, and 45 percent have tried at least three times.[21] Church could make a real difference. One study found that people who went to church weekly were 32 percent more likely to stop smoking than those who never went, while those who went to religious gatherings more than once per week were 40 percent more likely to quit.[22] The pastor of the church I went to when I was a student called the stories in his sermons "mental cigarette breaks." Little did he know that by attending church each week, the people in his congregation were a lot less likely to feel the need for literal cigarette breaks!

Church could also help you if you're struggling with alcohol or drug abuse. As we saw above, "deaths of despair" have surged in recent years, and many public health initiatives have tried to stem this tragic flow. But one of the best protections against dying from despair is church. One large-scale study found that women who attended services at least once per week have a 68 percent lower risk of death from despair than those who never attended; men who attended services at least once per week have a 33 percent lower risk.[23] Many of my neighbors in Cambridge, Massachusetts, think Christianity is bad for women. It turns out going to church each week has a disproportionately positive effect on women when it comes to the risks of drug and alcohol overdose or suicide.

But what if you're already following the seven keys to longevity advertised in the *New York Times*? Does that mean you don't need church? No. A six-year study of nearly four thousand older adults found that frequent religious attenders "reported greater social support, less depression, and better health practices (reduced smoking and alcohol consumption)" than those who didn't attend. But these constituent factors alone "were not sufficient to explain the relationship between religious attendance and longer survival."[24] Worshiping with others every week is life-and-health promoting.

Directions for Use

At ninety-one, Dorothy is the oldest member of our church. Resplendent in a pristine dress and hat, she lifts not only the average age in a church that trends quite young but also the average standard of attire. Originally from Jamaica and the mother of nine children, Dorothy walks to church each week, supported by her cane and her desire to worship with God's people. I want to be like Dorothy when I grow up. Following in her footsteps to church each week and joining in a midweek Bible study is my best hope of living to her age and only needing slight support to walk substantial distances. But church isn't just for the clean-living Dorothys among us.

Jesus often spent his time with the least-clean-living people of his day, and following his lead, our church works hard to be a place where those who struggle with smoking, alcohol, or drugs are loved and helped. Addiction expert Maia Szalavitz explains, "Americans aren't facing an addiction crisis because we get too much dopamine from overabundant cheap thrills. Our problem, instead, is a lack of connection, community and purpose."[25] A healthy church can give us the connection, purpose, and community we need, whether we struggle with alcohol, drugs, smoking, porn addiction, or doomscrolling social media. It can be the magic pill to help us turn away from other ecstasy-inducing or de-stressing pills. And because forgiveness is built into the motherboard of Christianity, a healthy church community will be right there for us each time we fail.

One friend in his sixties is breaking almost all the *New York Times*'s seven keys. He smokes, eats hardly any fruits and vegetables, sleeps little, and has struggled with an alcohol dependency for decades. He can go months, or even years, without a drink. But then something will trigger him to start again, and he ends up hospitalized. When this happens, it's our job as his church family to help him get back on his feet. Sometimes this takes multiple attempts. And, ultimately, it's only his faith in Jesus that can really dig him out when he falls down. One time, not long after this dear brother had come out of the hospital after a longer spell of drinking, I asked him what had made him stop. He just replied, "The Lord."

3

Moral Health Benefits

AS HE SET OUT TO WRITE his 2015 book *Bad Faith: When Religious Belief Undermines Modern Medicine*, Paul A. Offit, MD, assumed he would "sound the same themes that have been sounded by militant atheists like Richard Dawkins, Christopher Hitchens, and Sam Harris: that religion is illogical and potentially harmful." Offit was a professor of pediatrics at the University of Pennsylvania. He'd witnessed parents refusing the help their children needed for religious reasons, and he'd seen lives lost as a result. But after reading the Bible and researching history, Offit found his expectations scrambled. "Independent of whether you believe in the existence of God or that Jesus was the Son of God," Offit reflects, "you have to be impressed with the man described as Jesus of Nazareth." He goes on,

> At the time of Jesus' life, around 4 B.C. to 30 A.D., child abuse, as noted by one historian, was "the crying vice of the Roman Empire." Infanticide was common. Abandonment was common. . . . But Jesus stood up for children. Cared about them when those around him typically didn't.[1]

Today, we see infants and children as full human beings. But as Offit discovered, that wasn't true in the Greco-Roman empire.

> Children weren't considered to be people; they were property no different than slaves. So parents could do whatever they wanted to them. Children were stoned, beaten, flung into dung heaps, starved to death, traded for beds, sexually abused.

After researching the historic effects of Christianity, Offit came to this surprising view: "It is hard to overstate the [positive] influence of Jesus' teachings on the fate of children."[2]

You may have read this book thus far and thought, "OK, perhaps church is a force for good in terms of health and happiness for its adherents, but what about the harms done in the name of Christianity?" That's a fair question, and in this chapter, I'll seek to answer it. But first, I want to make the case that even our ideas about what counts as harm have come to us from Christianity—whether we realize it or not.

Diagnosis

If you look back through history and around the world today, you'll see a host of things that strike you as profoundly wrong. Offit mentioned some of them. Child abuse. Horrific violence. Enslavement. Starvation and oppression of the poor. Regardless of our views on God, we likely share a set of principles we see as universal moral truths. For instance, I'm guessing you believe all humans are innately valuable regardless of their sex, age, income, physical abilities, or racial heritage. I'm guessing you think we should help those trapped in poverty, that rape is morally repugnant, that infanticide is wrong, and that genocide is evil. Since most people in our culture—whether they identify as atheist, agnostic, Jewish, Christian, Muslim, Hindu, Buddhist, or nothing in particular—hold these truths to be self-evident, we see these views as basic moral common sense. But if we look at history, they're not.

Don't take my word for it.

When agnostic British historian Tom Holland set out to write *Dominion: How the Christian Revolution Remade the World*, he thought belief in universal human value and equality was the A-B-C of ethics, not dependent on any particular religion or philosophy. But like Offit, Holland changed his mind. His research showed that his core beliefs about universal value and equality were introduced and normalized across the West by Christianity. Their origins, as Holland puts it, "lay not in the French Revolution, nor in the Declaration of Independence, nor in the Enlightenment, but in the Bible."[3]

So, was Jesus just ahead of his time—like Copernicus and Galileo, who discovered that the earth revolves around the sun? Was Jesus's teaching about universal love and valuing the poor, sick, and oppressed merely an early-stage uncovering of moral truth that would've been discovered anyway? No. As Holland came to see, if we cut Jesus out of the equation, we won't find our feet on solid, secular foundations for our ethical beliefs. Rather, we're like someone "sitting on the great branch of Christianity, and sawing it off."[4]

Atheist historian and bestselling author Yuval Noah Harari makes the same point from a different angle. Quoting the Declaration of Independence, Harari observes that the Americans "got the idea of equality from Christianity" and points out that if we stop believing in the Bible's God, we don't have any ground for our convictions.[5] Some try to base a secular understanding of human equality on science. But as Harari points, out "belief in the unique worth and rights of human beings . . . has embarrassingly little in common with the scientific study of *Homo sapiens*."[6] Indeed, from his atheist perspective, Harari calls human rights "figments of our fertile imaginations."[7]

What does this mean for us?

It means that when we hear news from around the world and gasp with horror at the slaughtering, enslavement, and oppression we're witnessing, the air with which we gasp is Christian air. When we recoil at rape, child abuse, sex trafficking, and people being mired in abject poverty, we're grasping at the Bible's diagnostic tools to recognize these things as wrong. For Roman soldiers before Jesus's birth, slaughtering, enslaving, and oppressing people were all in a good day's work. What's more, this work was smiled upon by Greco-Roman gods. What we call rape and child abuse they'd call normal outlets for a man's libido. We think it's obvious that women are as valuable as men. But they thought women were clearly less valuable. We think sick and disabled people are equal in inherent worth to their able-bodied, healthy peers. But the ancients did not. We think the rich should help the poor. But as Holland notes, the Greek and Roman gods "cared nothing for the poor."[8]

It was Jesus's teachings (with deep roots in the fertile soil of the Old Testament) that placed the hungry, sick, and dispossessed right at the center of our ethical concern. It was

Jesus's valuing of women that lifted women to a place of equal worth with men. As historian Kyle Harper explains, it was Christian sexual ethics that cut Roman men off from their ability to sexually abuse those they enslaved and gave us the idea of sexual consent for women.[9] And as Offit discovered, it was Jesus's valuing of children that changed how we see children to this day.

But is this really so unique to Christianity?

You may have heard that all religions have a version of the golden rule—that you should treat others as you'd want them to treat you—so there's really nothing special about Christian ethics. But the question we must ask is "Who counts within the system?" In many ancient systems of belief, the "others" whom we should treat as we'd want them to treat us are those who share our beliefs, sex, nationality, or social status. But Jesus universalized the "other" we're to care for to include those *least* like us. After affirming that to "love your neighbor as yourself" encapsulates the moral law of the Hebrew Scriptures, Jesus was asked, "And who is my neighbor?" In response, he told a story of love extended to a racial and religious enemy who'd been robbed and left to bleed out on the road (Luke 10:25–37).

Without the moral anchor dropped by Jesus, we're left with "you do you." You could say, "I think all humans have inherent worth and value," just like I can say, "I think sushi is delicious." But you can't say everyone should think the same. Two years ago, I met an atheist professor at the Harvard School of Public Health whose research focuses on curbing the spread of infectious diseases. He told me how his work helps save the lives of vulnerable people in developing countries. I gently asked him if he knew his atheism didn't give him grounds for his belief in universal human value. He said that he did know.

If you're a nonreligious person, you may think, *That's precisely why I don't believe in God. My atheist friends care deeply for the poor and vulnerable while you Christians talk a good talk and do nothing.* It's not hard to find extremely loving atheists and morally repugnant people who identify as Christian. So, does the moral diagnostic of the Bible prove (ironically) that Christianity is false, because of all the wrongs done in Christ's name?

That's a fair question.

If we look back throughout the last two thousand years and all around the world today, we'll see many instances of supposed followers of Jesus slaughtering, oppressing, and abusing people. To be sure, some of these heinous acts were done by people falsely claiming to be Christians. Jesus warned that he'd always have fake followers. But other deeply sinful acts came from people who (as far as we can tell) were otherwise sincere in their faith. In *Bullies and Saints: An Honest Look at the Good and Evil of Christian History*, Australian historian John Dickson documents the moral highs and lows of those claiming to be Christians—and there are many lows. If the Bible taught that Christians are by definition good, the evils done by Christians would indeed disprove the Christian faith. But it doesn't.

The Bible doesn't claim that Christians are innately good. Instead, it teaches that we're rotten to the core—so bad that Jesus had to die to take the punishment for all our sin. Becoming an authentic follower of Jesus should certainly result in growing love for others and rejection of our natural, sinful tendences. But while the Bible promises complete forgiveness for our sins because of Jesus's death, it also teaches that Christians will continue to be sinners till the day we die. The lingering sinfulness of Christians doesn't prove the Christian message isn't true. It's actually one piece of evidence that Jesus's death was necessary. If my heart were basically good, I might need a great example to set me on the right path. But I wouldn't need the Son of God to die to take the punishment for all my sin. I might need a moral mentor. But I wouldn't need a crucified Messiah. No Christian lives up to the moral standards set by Jesus. But we need those self-same standards even to decry the history of Christian sin. So, did Jesus set a moral standard and then leave an army of his so-called followers who failed to follow him in any way? No. If the many moral failures of Christians give us pause, we must also take into account the extraordinary record of good done in Jesus's name.

Prescription

As Offit was surprised to find, Jesus's emphasis on caring for the poor, sick, and oppressed has spurred his followers to found hospitals and rescue orphans. It's led to abolition movements, poverty relief, and laws against forced sex. In the last two thousand years, Christians have been responsible for more self-sacrificing care for those in need than followers of any other faith or philosophical tradition. Jesus identifies so closely with those in need that he taught his followers that any time Christians care for "the least of these"—the hungry, thirsty, sick, imprisoned, or far from home—they're caring for him (Matt. 25:31–46). As skeptic of Christianity Bart Ehrman puts it, "The very idea that society should serve the poor, the sick, and the marginalized" is "a distinctively Christian concern," and without the spread of Christianity across the West, "we may well never have had institutionalized welfare for the poor or organized health care for the sick."[10]

Jesus-motivated love for those in need has struck even those most opposed to Christianity. When the fourth-century Roman Emperor Julian was trying to turn the empire back to Roman gods after the previous emperor had converted to Christianity, he wrote a letter to Arsacius, high priest of Galatia, grumbling that Christians "support not only their own poor but ours as well." Julian complained that his priests needed to raise their game in caring for the poor. But as Holland points out, this just shows how Christian thinking had seeped into this anti-Christian emperor's veins. The priests could've legitimately responded that nothing in their whole religious system had required them to support the poor!

What about today?

Many Westerners think Christians are all talk when it comes to those in need. But as atheist psychologist Jonathan Haidt points out, this simply isn't true. Noting this prejudice among his fellow atheists, Haidt writes,

> Surveys have long shown that religious believers in the United States are happier, healthier, longer-lived, and more generous to charity and to each other than are

secular people. Most of these effects have been documented in Europe too.[11]

Haidt goes on to urge his nonreligious readers to sit with this evidence. "If you believe that morality is about happiness and suffering," he argues, "then I think you are obligated to take a close look at the way religious people actually live and ask what they are doing right."

So, does all this charitable giving land in church budgets? No. "Religious believers give more money than secular folk to secular charities, and to their neighbors," Haidt observes. "They give more of their time, too, and of their blood. Even if you excuse secular liberals from charity because they vote for government welfare programs, it is awfully hard to explain why secular liberals give so little blood."[12] The idea that less religion means more generosity toward those most in need isn't supported by the data. As a 2019 report from the Philanthropy Roundtable puts it, "In study after study, religious practice is the behavioral variable with the strongest and most consistent association with generous giving." What's more, "Two thirds of people who worship at least twice a month give to secular causes, compared to less than half of nonattenders, and the average secular gift by a church attender is 20 percent bigger."[13]

The title of this book claims that going to church can literally save your life. But it's also true that countless people who don't go to church have had their lives saved by the generosity of those who do.

Evangelicals like me often get the worst press for their hypocrisy and lack of care for those in need. Sometimes, the attacks are warranted. But in an article titled "Evangelicals Without Blowhards," Pulitzer Prize–winning journalist Nicholas Kristof, who has devoted much of his career to covering humanitarian crises, points out that evangelical Christians "are disproportionately likely to donate 10 percent of their incomes to charities." Kristof challenges his readers,

> Go to the front lines, at home or abroad, in the battles against hunger, malaria, prison rape, obstetric fistula, human trafficking or genocide, and some of the bravest people you meet are evangelical Christians (or conservative Catholics, similar in many ways) who truly live their faith.[14]

If you, like Kristof, are a "not particularly religious" person who cares deeply about the plight of the most vulnerable around the world, you may want to take a closer look at Christianity.

Directions for Use

In his 2019 book *Outgrowing God: A Beginner's Guide*, new atheist author Richard Dawkins grudgingly acknowledges the evidence that people who believe in God behave better, on average, than their unbelieving peers. He says he finds it rather patronizing to the unenlightened masses to say to his readers, "Of course you and I are too intelligent to believe in God, but we think it would be a good idea if *other* people did!"[15] Yet this is one logical conclusion from the data. If, like Dawkins, you think you're too intelligent to believe in God, you might not want to go to church yourself. But in the interest of the common good—especially the good of those in need—you'll have to hope that other people do.

But this isn't a consistent place to land.

As we saw earlier, Offit claimed that "independent of whether you believe in the existence of God or that Jesus was the Son of God . . . you have to be impressed with the man described as Jesus of Nazareth."[16] But, actually, you don't. If Jesus isn't the Creator God of all the universe made flesh, we have no underlying reason to believe his teachings about universal human value. We might as well live selfishly. If we're no more than complex biomedical machines wandering around a minor planet orbiting one of a countless host of suns in a completely pointless universe, then murder, rape, and child abuse are just shifting configurations of atoms and molecules. Our value and our values are not real. They are, as Harari puts it, “figments of our fertile imaginations.” So if we want to cling to human worth, it’s worth asking, “Is there any chance that Christianity is true?” That’s the question we’ll explore in chapter 4.

4

Spiritual Health Benefits

"I THINK THERE'S a 50 percent chance you have cancer."

This wasn't the answer I'd expected. My first routine mammogram had flagged some questionable tissue. When I showed up for a diagnostic biopsy, I asked the doctor for her best guess on whether I had cancer. When she told me it was fifty-fifty, I was startled. I'd expected a much lower probability. In the week following, as I waited for results, I had to reckon, for the first time in my life, with the possibility that I was terminally ill.

Unlike most humans throughout history, we're now enabled by our medical advances to insulate ourselves from the reality of death. We know deep down we're going to die, but we can choose to block our ears to that insistent siren, at least while it's in the distance. At some point, however, it'll get so loud we can't pretend we haven't heard. Someone we deeply love will die. Or we'll hear a doctor tell us we have cancer. In a review of research on the benefits of going to church, VanderWeele states the painfully obvious: "Religious participation of course does not protect against 'death' itself."[1]

So, what should we make of the unpalatable fact that we will die?

The late physicist Stephen Hawking, who lived with motor neuron disease throughout his adult life, described mortality like this: "I regard the brain as a computer which will stop working when its components fail." In Hawking's view, that was simply that. "There is no heaven or afterlife for broken down computers," he went on; "that is a fairy story for people afraid of the dark."[2] So, is this how all highly educated, scientifically minded adults in the modern world should think? Have the advances in the sum of human knowledge that gave us modern medicine simultaneously robbed us of belief in something after death?

I don't think so.

Professor VanderWeele is a world-class epidemiologist with multiple degrees in subjects ranging from mathematics to philosophy, from universities including Harvard and Oxford. And as he puts it, "Christianity is not simply a matter of weak-minded individuals gullibly believing a series of nonsensical stories. There is serious evidence that lends substantial credibility to the Christian faith."[3] In this chapter, we will scratch the surface of that evidence—the evidence that filled my lungs with hope when I was told I had a fifty-fifty chance of cancer. We'll look at a central truth claim of the Christian faith: that Jesus is the doctor we all desperately need.

Diagnosis

When I went for my initial mammogram, I felt great. I had no reason to suspect I might have cancer. But the cruelty of cancer is that you can feel just fine while your body starts to trudge along the path to death. We need experts with machines to look inside us and assess our health. And like an expert radiologist, Jesus offers us a diagnosis of our spiritual state whether we feel sick or not.

If you pick up a Bible and start to read the New Testament, the first book you'll read is Matthew's Gospel. If you get as far as chapter 9, you'll come to the part where Matthew shares how he met Jesus. Like Jesus, Matthew was Jewish. But unlike Jesus, Matthew was a tax collector, working for the Roman overlords to gather taxes from his fellow Jews. The tax collectors were hated by their fellow countrymen. They profited from the exploitation of their own people and typically extorted extra cash to line their own pockets, so they were shunned by other Jews. But strangely, Jesus called Matthew to be one of his core followers, and even more strangely, Matthew left his tax collector booth and followed Jesus.

When Jesus went to dinner at Matthew's house, "many tax collectors and sinners" came to the dinner too (Matt. 9:10). A group of ardently religious Jews known as the Pharisees were horrified. They asked Jesus's disciples, "Why does your teacher eat with tax collectors and sinners?" (Matt. 9:11). It was a fair question. Jesus was supposed to have been sent by God. And here he was surrounded by the most notoriously sinful people of his day. In our terms, it would be like a famous pastor walking straight into the sketchiest casino in Las Vegas.

Jesus's response to the Pharisees' critique is striking: "Those who are well have no need of a physician, but those who are sick [need one]. Go and learn what this means: 'I desire mercy, and not sacrifice.' For I came not to call the righteous, but sinners" (Matt. 9:12–13). Jesus has a point. It's when we're struck with cancer that we need a doctor, not when we're well. If Jesus is the spiritual doctor sent by God, he didn't come for people who are good but for the morally diseased. The tax collectors were the spiritual lepers of their day: their sickness was on show for all to see. But Jesus's comment about mercy leaves us with a nagging question, *What about the Pharisees?*

I wonder where you see yourself in Matthew's story. I don't know whether you believe there's a God who made the universe or not. But if we imagine for a moment that there is, I wonder if you think that God would see you as a "righteous" or "good" person? Not perfect, certainly. But maybe (like the Pharisees) you see yourself as good enough to be on the right side of God.

Or maybe you identify more with the tax collectors. Perhaps you have a sneaking fear that if there's a God who judges human lives, you might be in his bad books. That was how my best friend, Rachel, felt when she first became convinced that God exists. She was an undergrad at Yale University, and an atheist. But one day, as Rachel sat reading a book about Christianity in the library, she suddenly became convinced that God is real. It was a terrifying moment. She knew that she was sinful. She was greedy, selfish, mean, deceitful, irreligious, and sexually immoral—she'd even stolen the book on Christianity that she was reading! Rachel was a straight-up tax collector. But if you read through Matthew's Gospel—or the other three biographies of Jesus's life included in the Bible—you'll find that Jesus's diagnosis of our spiritual state is bad news not just for the tax collector types like Rachel but also for the most clean-living, seemingly religious citizens. Alarmingly, like a sophisticated imaging device that sees through all our outer layers, Jesus diagnoses spiritual cancer deep in all our hearts (Mark 7:20–23).

You may be thinking, *Listen, I'm not perfect. But I'm not a spiritual cancer case! I get why murderers, rapists, and people like that might face God's judgment. But I'm not like them.* According to Jesus, however, you and I aren't as unlike the murderers as we might think. "You have heard that it was said to those of old, 'You shall not murder,' " Jesus declared. "But I say to you that everyone who is angry with his brother will be liable to judgment" (Matt. 5:21–22). We may not express our anger with the violent extreme of murder. But when you hear the stories of the kinds of people who do kill, you begin to entertain the uncomfortable thought that if you'd lived their life, you might have chosen murder too. The global bestseller *The Secret History* tells the story of a group of college students who conspire in cold blood to murder one of their best friends. The narrator (one of the same students) tells us he doesn't think of himself as a bad person, and as we walk step-by-step with him toward the murder, we see how he got there and wonder if we would've trod that path as well.

Likewise, we may hear about harmful sexual behavior and think, *I'm not like that.* But Jesus says that if we take an honest look inside our hearts, we'll find we're not so different. "You have heard that it was said, 'You shall not commit adultery,' "

Jesus told his first disciples. "But I say to you that everyone who looks at a woman with lustful intent has already committed adultery with her in his heart" (Matt. 5:27–28). If there's a God who sees what happens in my heart—the selfishness, meanness, greed, shameful desires, petty jealousies, and lack of care for others' suffering—it's not surprising that he diagnoses me as spiritually sick. But instead of just discarding me as not worth salvaging, Jesus claims he's the doctor who has come from God to help the most diseased.

According to the Bible, our greatest danger isn't that we'll die in some horrific accident or from a crippling disease. It's that we'll face the righteous judgment of the God who made the universe. Our greatest need isn't for health and wellness in this life so we can stave off death as long as possible. It's for a Savior who can take God's judgment for our sin upon himself and walk us right through death to everlasting life and love beyond the grave.

You may be thinking, *Stop right there. You can't expect me to believe there is a God who made the universe!* Some famous scientists claim that science has disproved creation. "There is no God," wrote Stephen Hawking in his final book. "No one created the universe and no one directs our fate."[4] But for every famous scientist who espouses atheism, I could point you to another world-class scientist in the same field who is a follower of Jesus. For instance, one of Hawking's closest collaborators at Cambridge, Paul Shellard, is a convinced Christian. As another Cambridge physics professor, Russell Cowburn, explains, "Understanding more of science doesn't make God smaller. It allows us to see his creative activity in more detail."[5]

If we look back at history, we'll find that what we now call science was first developed by people who believed in the God revealed in the Bible. Just as our deep belief in universal human value is best grounded by belief in the God who gave us moral laws, so the existence of one God who made the universe according to consistent laws is the first and best foundation for the scientific method.

Some people think that because scientists seek natural (rather than supernatural) causes for natural phenomena, this means science is a signpost to atheism. But as Princeton philosopher of science Hans Halvorson explains, the project of science is to figure out the laws and principles on which the universe runs—like working out the blueprint of a house. If you managed to reconstruct the architectural design on which your house was built, you wouldn't expect to see the outline of the architect in the design, nor would you think the absence of that outline disproved the existence of the architect.[6] The architect is the creator of the blueprint, not part of the building!

So let's imagine for a moment that there's a God who made the universe. How can we say that Jesus is the one true revelation of that God? Many people think that (unlike scientific truths) religious claims are more like tastes. Just as different cultures enjoy different foods, the thinking goes, so Jesus can be "true for me but not for you." But Jesus is too awkwardly exclusive, too radically inclusive, and too stubbornly objective for this approach to work.

First, Jesus is awkwardly exclusive. He claims not just that he is one way to a relationship with God but that he is the only way, the truth, and the life (John 14:6). If you believe that Jesus is just one of many paths to God, you're flatly contradicting Jesus. Like an awkward dinner guest, the Jesus of the Gospels won't take his equal place at the religious table. He'll stop storms, heal the sick, raise the dead, and eat with sinners. But he won't fit in with modern platitudes about all world religions being one.

Second, Jesus is too radically inclusive. Instead of being tied to a particular culture or ethnicity, Jesus has billions of followers spread across the world—in Asia, Africa, North and South America, Europe, and Australia. The Christian church is both the world's largest and its most diverse religious group, cutting across all barriers of race, geography, and culture.[7] So Jesus's claims can't be limited to just one people group or quadrant of the world, because the Christian movement has been multicultural and multiethnic from the first. I know multiple professors at world-class universities who were raised with different religious backgrounds—Jewish, Hindu, Muslim, Buddhist—but are now convinced Jesus is the only way to be made right with God. To say all religions teach the same thing isn't respectful of the followers of different world religions. It's ultimately disrespectful because it depends on not taking the distinct claims of any world religion seriously.

Third, the claims of Christianity are stubbornly objective. The truth of Christianity depends on a historical event: the bodily resurrection of Jesus from the dead. You may think it's impossible for modern educated people to believe someone rose from death two thousand years ago. But it isn't. In the summer of 2022, history professor and journalist Molly Worthen became a Christian. She'd been challenged by a pastor she interviewed to investigate the evidence for Jesus's resurrection. After many months of reading books and checking footnotes, Worthen came to the conclusion that the resurrection makes the best sense of the evidence. She also realized that if this is true, it changes everything. She couldn't just sit on the sidelines. If Jesus had defeated death, he'd also won the right to her allegiance.

Don't get me wrong. It certainly takes faith to recognize that a first-century Jewish rabbi broke through death and is the rightful Lord of all the universe. But it isn't a faith untethered from the evidence. Right now, I'm flying in a plane to California. When I got on this plane, it was an act of faith. I'm trusting my life to the pilot and the engineers who built the plane. My faith could be misplaced. We just had some major turbulence, and my daughter (who is traveling with me) was scared the plane would crash. I reassured her it wouldn't. But sometimes planes do fall out of the sky. It's possible I'm wrong to reassure her. But I have ample evidence to believe we're safe in this metallic tube with wings and that it will get us from Boston to Los Angeles. If I went back two thousand years, however, and asked someone to sit inside a massive, hollow lump of metal with the expectation that it would take off and fly above the clouds, they'd have thought I was insane—or counting on a miracle. Today you'd think me a little odd to *not* believe planes can fly.

Some people think Jesus's claims have become less and less believable with time. Sure, people in the ancient world could buy the story of a human who was also God and who rose from the dead, but we know better. In fact, if anything, the claims of Jesus have become *more* credible since he first made them.

When Jesus died on a Roman cross, he had just a few dozen followers. He'd claimed he was the great King whom God had promised to send to the Jewish people. But instead of being crowned, he'd been killed. A reasonable observer might have thought this little Jewish sect would fizzle out—extinguished like a cigarette by Rome. But it didn't. Jesus never ruled an empire, raised an army, or even wrote a book. Most of his followers were poor. They weren't the power brokers of their day. And yet, the Christian movement spread like wildfire after Jesus's death, and it's been growing ever since.

Today, almost a third of humans all across the globe claim to be Christians. Jesus's teachings have shaped what even many who identify as atheist believe about morality and universal human worth. His followers birthed modern science. His four first-century biographies and the letters written by his first disciples have become the bestselling books of all time. His claim that anyone who wants to follow him must care for those in need has led to more provision and protection for the poor, oppressed, and suffering than any other influence. At the end of Matthew's Gospel, Jesus tells his followers, "All authority in heaven and on earth has been given to me" (Matt. 28:18). Two thousand years later, that claim looks, if anything, *more* plausible.

So if it's not unreasonable to think Jesus is the doctor sent by God, and if his diagnosis is that we're all spiritually sick, what medication does he offer?

Prescription

When my friend Rachel was first jolted into the belief that God is real and that he has the right to judge her actions, thoughts, and words, she was completely terrified. This is the bad news of the Christian faith, the stage-four cancer diagnosis. But moments later, she was struck by the extraordinary offer Jesus makes. This great physician doesn't merely pop a magic pill into our hands and wish us luck. He takes our moral sickness on himself and gives his life in place of ours. As Jesus explained to his first followers, although he was the great King sent by God, he "came not to be served but to serve, and to give his life as a ransom for many" (Matt. 20:28). When Jesus died on a Roman cross, he took the punishment we deserve so anyone who trusts in him could be forgiven and eternally embraced by God. He drained his blood to fill our veins. He breathed his last to fill our lungs. He suffered the most horrifying death so we could live the most ecstatic life with him forever, if we trust in him.

This offer is extended as a gift. But we must take it. It's not the healthy who need a doctor, but the sick, and we must recognize our spiritual sickness if we're going to put our case in Jesus's hands. If you think you're spiritually well, you won't see Jesus's offer as good news. But if you know deep down that anyone who saw your darkest, meanest, most unpalatable thoughts would run from you, then you might just be ready to go running into Jesus's outstretched arms.

Directions for Use

I asked you on the first page of this book to imagine you were seeing pills instead of pages. Then, I made the case that going to church each week could function like a set of pills to make you happier, healthier, and longer-lived. But in the end, you could attend church all your life and live to ninety-five and never take the pill that really counts.

That pill is hard to swallow. It requires us to let go of our pride and recognize our need. But if we face up to the fact that we're far worse than we imagined, we will also have the eyes to see how radically we're loved. The doctor who can diagnose the moral cancer in our hearts is the same Son of God who came to earth to take the punishment for all our sin upon himself. If we decide to trust in him, we do not need to fear when cancer comes for us, or when our car spins out of our control, or when our heart starts sputtering to an exhausted halt. This Jesus didn't only pay the price for sin. He also conquered death—the enemy we can't defeat, however much we elongate our lives with healthy practices.

My biopsy results came back all clear. But when death comes for me, I won't need to be scared, because I know the great physician has already taken up my case. The day my heart stops beating, I will fall into the arms of Jesus, who alone can carry me through death to everlasting, resurrection life with him.

That offer's on the table for you too. The pill is there for you to swallow. No other medication in this world will do you good when you come face-to-face with death. But if you put your trust in Jesus, who has faced the worst imaginable death for sinful people just like you and me, you'll find that all he has for you eternally is life and love beyond your wildest dreams.

So, will you take the pill?

Notes

Introduction

1. Tyler J. VanderWeele and John Siniff, "Religion May Be a Miracle Drug," *USA Today*, October 28, 2016, https://www.usatoday.com/.
2. Michael Graham, Jim Davis, and Ryan Burge, *The Great Dechurching: Who's Leaving, Why Are They Going, and What Will It Take to Bring Them Back?* (Zondervan Reflective, 2023).
3. VanderWeele and Siniff, "Religion May Be a Miracle Drug."

Chapter 1: Mental Health Benefits

1. Dan Witters, "U.S. Depression Rates Reach New Highs," *Gallup*, May 17, 2023, https://news.gallup.com/.
2. Dan Witters, "U.S. Depression Rates."
3. Preeti Vankar, "Percentage of U.S. Youths with a Major Depressive Episode in the Past Year from 2004 to 2023, by Gender," *Statista*, November 4, 2024, https://www.statista.com/.
4. Derek Thompson, "Why American Teens Are So Sad," *The Atlantic*, April 11, 2022, https://www.theatlantic.com/.
5. Sally C. Curtin and Matthew F. Garnett, "Suicide and Homicide Death Rates Among Youth and Young Adults Aged 10–24: United States, 2001–2021," National Center for Health Statistics

data brief, no. 471, Centers for Disease Control and Prevention, June 15, 2023, https://stacks.cdc.gov/view/cdc/128423.

6. Renee D. Goodwin, Lisa C. Dierker, Melody Wu, Sandro Galea, Christina W. Hoven, and Andrea H. Weinberger, "Trends in U.S. Depression Prevalence from 2015 to 2020: The Widening Treatment Gap," *American Journal of Preventive Medicine* 63, no. 5 (2022): 726–33, https://doi.org/10.1016/j.amepre.2022.05.014.
7. "Social Media and Youth Mental Health: The U.S. Surgeon General's Advisory," Office of the U.S. Surgeon General, https://www.hhs.gov/, pdf.
8. See, for example, Tyree Oredein and Cristine Delnevo, "The Relationship Between Multiple Sexual Partners and Mental Health in Adolescent Females," *Journal of Community Medicine and Health Education* 3, no. 7 (2013), https://www.researchgate.net/, and Sandhya Ramrakha, Charlotte Paul, Melanie L. Bell, Nigel Dickson, Terrie E. Moffitt, and Avshalom Caspi, "The Relationship Between Multiple Sex Partners and Anxiety, Depression, and Substance Dependence Disorders: A Cohort Study," *Archives of Sexual Behavior* 42, no. 5 (2013): 863–72, https://pubmed.ncbi.nlm.nih.gov/.
9. Sam Peltzman, "The Socio Political Demography of Happiness," George J. Stigler Center for the Study of the Economy and the State, working paper no. 331, July 12, 2023, https://ssrn.com/.
10. Kevin Wallsten, "Less Marriage, Worse Mental Health: The 'Marriage Advantage' in Mental Well-Being," Institute for Family Studies, March 6, 2024, https://ifstudies.org/blog/.
11. See Tyler J. VanderWeele, Tracy A. Balboni, and Howard K. Koh, "Invited Commentary: Religious Service Attendance and Implications for Clinical Care, Community Participation, and Public Health," *American Journal of Epidemiology* 191, no. 1 (2022): 31–35, https://academic.oup.com/. See also Bert Garssen, Anja

Visser, and Grieteke Pool, "Does Spirituality or Religion Positively Affect Mental Health? Meta-Analysis of Longitudinal Studies," *International Journal for the Psychology of Religion* 31, no. (2021), https://doi.org/10.1080/10508619.2020.1729570.

12. Tyler J. VanderWeele, "Religion and Health: A Synthesis," in *Spirituality and Religion Within the Culture of Medicine: From Evidence to Practice*, ed. Michael J. Balboni and John R. Peteet (Oxford University Press, 2017), 357–401.
13. Tyler J. VanderWeele, Shanshan Li, Alexander C. Tsai, and Ichiro Kawachi, "Association Between Religious Service Attendance and Lower Suicide Rates Among US Women," *JAMA Psychology* 73, no. 8 (2016), https://doi.org/10.1001/jamapsychiatry.2016.1243.
14. VanderWeele, Balboni, and Koh, "Religious Service Attendance," 33.
15. "Across 25 other countries for which data are available, actives report being happier than the unaffiliated by a statistically significant margin in almost half (12 countries), and happier than inactively religious adults in roughly one-third (nine) of the countries. The gaps are often striking. . . . And there is no country in which the data show that actives are significantly less happy than others." See "Religion's Relationship to Happiness, Civic Engagement, and Health Around the World," Pew Research Center, January 31, 2019, https://www.pewresearch.org/.
16. W. J. Strawbridge, S. J. Shema, R. D. Cohen, and G. A. Kaplan, "Religious Attendance Increases Survival by Improving and Maintaining Good Health Behaviors, Mental Health, and Social Relationships," *Annals of Behavioral Medicine* 23, no. 1 (2001): 68–74, https://doi.org/10.1207/s15324796abm2301_10.
17. Tyler VanderWeele, "Why Public Health Should Attend to the Spiritual Side of Life," *Harvard Public Health*, April 10, 2024, https://harvardpublichealth.org/.

18. Erica Komisar, "Don't Believe in God? Lie to Your Children," *Wall Street Journal*, December 5, 2019, https://www.wsj.com/.
19. Ying Chen, Eric S. Kim, Howard K. Koh, A. Lindsay Frazier, and Tyler J. VanderWeele, "Sense of Mission and Subsequent Health and Well-Being Among Young Adults: An Outcome-Wide Analysis," *American Journal of Epidemiology* 188, no. 4 (2019): 664–73, https://pubmed.ncbi.nlm.nih.gov/.
20. Lance D. Erickson and James W. Phillips, "The Effect of Religious-Based Mentoring on Educational Attainment: More Than Just a Spiritual High?," *Journal for the Scientific Study of Religion* 51, no. 3 (2012), https://doi.org/10.1111/j.1468-5906.2012.01661.x.
21. "Religious Upbringing Linked to Better Health and Well-Being During Early Adulthood," Harvard T. H. Chan School of Public Health, September 13, 2018, https://www.hsph.harvard.edu/.
22. "11 Reasons Spurgeon Was Depressed," The Spurgeon Center, July 11, 2017, https://www.spurgeon.org/.

Chapter 2: Physical Health Benefits

1. Dana G. Smith, "The 7 Keys to Longevity," *New York Times*, January 4, 2024, https://www.nytimes.com/.
2. Robert H. Shmerling, "Why Life Expectancy in the US is Falling," Harvard Health Publishing, October 20, 2022, https://www.health.harvard.edu/.
3. "Life Expectancy in the U.S. Declined a Year and a Half in 2020," National Center for Health Statistics, July 21, 2021, https://www.cdc.gov/.
4. "New Surgeon General Advisory Raises Alarm About the Devastating Impact of the Epidemic of Loneliness and Isolation in the United States," U.S. Department of Health and Human Services, May 3, 2023, https://www.hhs.gov/about/news/2023/05/03/new-surgeon-general-advisory-raises-alarm-about-devastating-impact-epidemic-loneliness-isolation-united-states.html.

5. Catherine Milner, "Britain Is in a Loneliness Epidemic—and Young People Are at the Heart of It," *Telegraph*, February 29, 2024, https://www.telegraph.co.uk/.
6. "New Surgeon General Advisory Raises Alarm."
7. "Our Epidemic of Loneliness and Isolation," Department of Health and Human Services (2023), 16, https://www.hhs.gov/, pdf.
8. "Cancer," Centers for Disease Control, October 13, 2023, https://www.cdc.gov/tobacco/campaign/tips/diseases/cancer.html.
9. "How Smoking Affects the Heart and Blood Vessels," National Heart, Lung, and Blood Institute, March 24, 2022, https://www.nhlbi.nih.gov/.
10. Rafael Meza, Pianpian Cao, Jihyoun Jeon, Kenneth E. Warner, and David T. Levy, "Trends in US Adult Smoking Prevalence, 2011 to 2022," *JAMA Health Forum* 4, no. 12 (2023), https://doi.org/10.1001/jamahealthforum.2023.4213.
11. As one report explains, "In 2000, there were 22.7 deaths of despair per 100,000 Americans. . . . By 2017, the rate had doubled to 45.8 per 100,000." "Long-Term Trends in Deaths of Despair," Social Capital Project report no. 4-19 (2019), https://www.jec.senate.gov/, pdf.
12. The rate increased from 10.7 deaths per one hundred thousand in 2001 to 14.1 in 2021. See Matthew F. Garnett and Sally C. Curtin, "Suicide Mortality in the United States, 2001–2021," Centers for Disease Control, April 2023, https://www.cdc.gov/.
13. "Understanding the Opioid Overdose Epidemic," Centers for Disease Control, April 5, 2024, https://www.cdc.gov/.
14. "Drug Overdose Deaths: Facts and Figures," National Institute on Drug Abuse, https://nida.nih.gov/.
15. Cara Poland, "Alcohol-Related Deaths Are Spiking. So Why Don't We Take Alcohol Addiction More Seriously?," Association of American Medical Colleges, March 20, 2024, https://www.aamc.org/.

16. Poland, "Alcohol-Related Deaths."
17. R. A. Hummer, R. G. Rogers, C. B. Nam, and C. G. Ellison, "Religious Involvement and U.S. Adult Mortality," *Demography* 36, no. 2 (1999): 273–85, https://pubmed.ncbi.nlm.nih.gov/.
18. VanderWeele cites a study that reported mortality odds ratios as follows: physical activity OR = 0.67; tobacco smoking cessation OR = 0.71; beta-blocker–congestive heart failure OR = 0.72; screening for mammography OR = 0.74; fruit and vegetable consumption OR = 0.74; service attendance OR = 0.75. (An odds ratio greater than 1 suggests that the exposure increases the odds of the outcome, while an odds ratio less than 1 indicates that the exposure decreases the odds of the outcome.) Tyler J. VanderWeele, "Religion and Health: A Synthesis," in *Spirituality and Religion Within the Culture of Medicine: From Evidence to Practice*, ed. Michael J. Balboni and John R. Peteet (Oxford University Press, 2017), 360. See also Giancarlo Lucchetti, Alessandra L. G. Lucchetti, and Harold G. Koenig, "Impact of Spirituality/Religiosity on Mortality: Comparison with Other Health Interventions," *Explore* 7, no. 4 (2011): 234–38, https://doi.org/10.1016/j.explore.2011.04.005.
19. Shanshan Li, Meir J. Stampfer, David R. Williams, and Tyler J. VanderWeele, "Association of Religious Service Attendance with Mortality Among Women," *JAMA Internal Medicine* 176, no. 6 (2016): 777–85, https://jamanetwork.com/.
20. VanderWeele, "Religion and Health," 360. See note 18 above.
21. Frank Newport, "Most U.S. Smokers Want to Quit, Have Tried Multiple Times," Gallup, July 31, 2013, https://news.gallup.com/.
22. Qiana L. Brown et al., "The Influence of Religious Attendance on Smoking," *Substance Use and Misuse* 49, no. 11 (2014): 1392–99, https://doi.org/10.3109/10826084.2014.912224.

23. Ying Chen, Howard K. Koh, Ichiro Kawachi, Michael Botticelli, and Tyler J. VanderWeele, "Religious Service Attendance and Deaths Related to Drugs, Alcohol, and Suicide Among US Health Care Professionals," *JAMA Psychiatry* 77, no. 7 (2020): 737–44, https://jamanetwork.com/.
24. Harold G. Koenig et al., "Does Religious Attendance Prolong Survival? A Six-Year Follow-Up Study of 3,968 Older Adults," *Journal of Gerontology*: *Medical Sciences* 54A, 7 (1999): M368–M376, https://pubmed.ncbi.nlm.nih.gov/.
25. Maia Szalavitz, "A 'Dopamine Fast' Will Not Save You from Addiction," *New York Times*, September 13, 2024, https://www.nytimes.com/.

Chapter 3: Moral Health Benefits

1. Paul A. Offit, "Why I Wrote This Book: Paul A. Offit, M.D., *Bad Faith: When Religious Belief Undermines Modern Medicine*," Casetext, May 17, 2015, https://casetext.com/.
2. Paul A. Offit, *Bad Faith: When Religious Belief Undermines Modern Medicine* (Basic, 2015), 127.
3. Tom Holland, *Dominion: How the Christian Revolution Remade the World* (Basic, 2021), 494.
4. Tom Holland (@holland_tom), "This—for fans of humanists sitting on the great branch of Christianity, and sawing it off for thoroughly Christian reasons—is pretty much the full bingo-card," X, December 23, 2022, 7:21 a.m., https://x.com/holland_tom/status/1606263821651288064.
5. Yuval Noah Harari, *Sapiens: A Brief History of Humankind* (HarperCollins, 2015), 109.
6. Harari, *Sapiens*, 253.
7. Harari, *Sapiens*, 32.
8. Holland, *Dominion*, 138.

9. Kyle Harper, *From Shame to Sin: The Christian Transformation of Sexual Morality in Late Antiquity* (Harvard University Press, 2013).
10. Bart Ehrman, *The Triumph of Christianity: How a Forbidden Religion Swept the World* (Simon and Schuster, 2018), 6.
11. Jonathan Haidt, "Moral Psychology and the Misunderstanding of Religion," Edge, September 21, 2007, https://www.edge.org/.
12. Haidt, "Moral Psychology."
13. Karl Zinsmeister, "Less God, Less Giving? Religion and Generosity Feed Each Other in Fascinating Ways," *Philanthropy Roundtable*, Winter 2019, https://www.philanthropyroundtable.org/.
14. Nicholas Kristof, "Evangelicals Without Blowhards," *New York Times*, July 30, 2011, https://www.nytimes.com/.
15. Richard Dawkins, *Outgrowing God: A Beginner's Guide* (Random House, 2019), 122.
16. Offit, "Why I Wrote This Book."

Chapter 4: Spiritual Health Benefits

1. Tyler J. VanderWeele, "Religion and Health: A Synthesis," in *Spirituality and Religion Within the Culture of Medicine: From Evidence to Practice*, ed. Michael J. Balboni and John R. Peteet (Oxford University Press, 2017), 359.
2. Ian Sample, "Stephen Hawking: 'There Is No Heaven; It's a Fairy Story,'" *Guardian*, May 15, 2011, https://www.theguardian.com/.
3. Tyler J. VanderWeele, "Knowledge Beyond Science? Assessing the Evidence for the Christian Faith," lecture presented at Indiana University, October 29, 2017, https://hfh.fas.harvard.edu/sites/projects.iq.harvard.edu/files/pik/files/sciencechristianity.pdf.
4. Stephen Hawking, Eddie Redmayne, Kip S. Thorne, and Lucy Hawking, *Brief Answers to the Big Questions* (John Murray, 2020), 38.
5. Russell Cowburn @veritasforum, "Understanding more of science doesn't make God smaller. It allows us to see his creative activity

in more detail," X, March 28, 2017, 3:01 p.m., https://x.com/veritasforum/status/846799483648327682.

6. Hans Halvorson, "Why Methodological Naturalism?," September 2, 2014, https://joelvelasco.net/teaching/2330/halvorson_methodological_naturalism.pdf.
7. "The Future of World Religions: Population Growth Projections, 2010–2050," Pew Research Center, April 2, 2015, https://www.pewresearch.org/religion/2015/04/02/religious-projections-2010-2050/.

Index

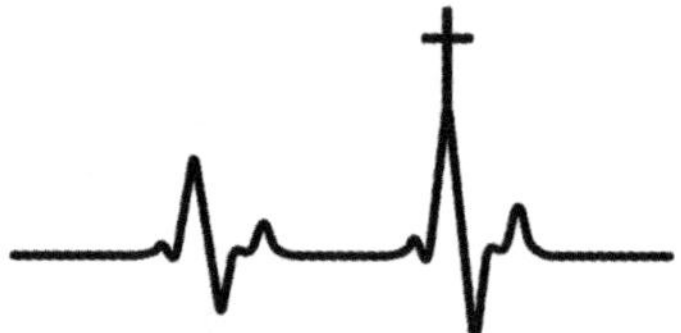

Find Your Church

To connect with a church in your area and see a list of questions frequently asked by those considering going to a new church, please scan the QR code below.

TGC THE GOSPEL COALITION

The Gospel Coalition (TGC) exists to renew and unify the contemporary church in the ancient gospel by declaring, defending, and applying the good news of Jesus to all of life.

Guided by a Council of more than 40 pastors in the Reformed tradition, TGC seeks to foster a mighty movement of spiritual renewal. We want to see God bless local churches with a gospel-centered ministry that fully integrates corporate worship, expository preaching, joyful obedience to God's Word, effective evangelism, loving community, and faithful engagement in the world.

We do this by producing content (including articles, podcasts, videos, courses, books, and curricula) and convening leaders (including conferences, cohorts, regional chapters, and international coalitions).

Join us by visiting TGC.org.

TGC.org